IMAGES
of America

CUDAHY

WISCONSIN

GENERATIONS OF PRIDE

CITY OF CUDAHY ANNEXATION MAP

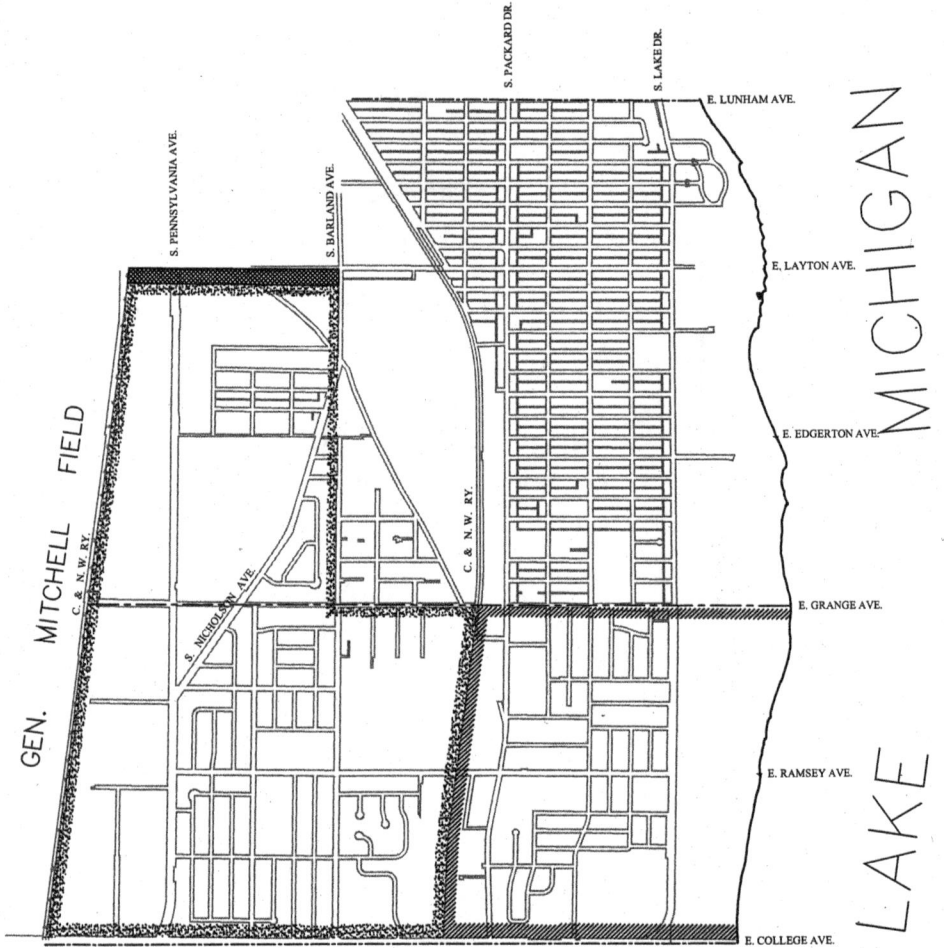

S. PACKARD DR.

S. LAKE DR.

E. LUNHAM AVE.

S. PENNSYLVANIA AVE.

S. BARLAND AVE.

E. LAYTON AVE.

MICHIGAN

MITCHELL FIELD

C. & N. W. RY.

C. & N. W. RY.

S. NICHOLSON AVE.

E. EDGERTON AVE.

E. GRANGE AVE.

GEN.

E. RAMSEY AVE.

LAKE

E. COLLEGE AVE.

AREA

Village	1895	....	1231.80 Ac.
City	1906	....	1231.80 Ac.
Annex.	1949	....	582.40 Ac.
Annex.	1952	....	1216.48 Ac.
Annex.	1954	....	14.44 Ac.
Total Area		....	3045.12 Ac.
			4.76 Sq. Miles

LEGEND

Boundaries 1949 Annexation
Boundaries 1952 Annexation
Area Annexed in 1954

(Map courtesy of Cudahy Engineering Department.)

IMAGES
of America

CUDAHY

WISCONSIN

GENERATIONS OF PRIDE

Joan Paul

ARCADIA
PUBLISHING

Published by Arcadia Publishing
Charleston, South Carolina

Library of Congress Catalog Card Number: 2001098153

For all general information contact Arcadia Publishing at:
Telephone 843-853-2070
Fax 843-853-0044
E-mail sales@arcadiapublishing.com
For customer service and orders:
Toll-Free 1-888-313-2665

Visit us on the Internet at www.arcadiapublishing.com

Acknowledgments

I wish to thank everyone who had some part in preparation of this book. First and foremost, thank you to all who provided pictures—for without them there would be no book—and to the many persons who, over the years, contributed photos to the Cudahy Historical Society files, which were used extensively for this project. A very special thanks to the Cudahy Public Library for allowing the Society to copy valuable contents from its local history file many years ago. Much appreciation to Mayor Raymond Glowacki for his support, City Attorney Robert Jursik for legal advice, City Engineer Craig Faucett for the map on page 2, and City assessor Steve Minor for information on the city's progress. Thanks to those who helped identify persons, event, or dates: Mary Becker, Joe Buichl, Irma Henry, Bob Houlehen, Ken Joslin, Larry Lezala, Marion Marino, Tom Paul, Gerald Ponec, Mary Salvatore, Joe Scaffidi, Bill and Petie Schroettner, Frank Taucher, Jack Vaccaro, Bess Waters, and particularly Charlie Wolbert who went the extra mile. Thank you to my daughters: Kathy Lorum for the use of her computer and Jean Madaus for proofreading services.

Proceeds from the sale of this book will go to the Cudahy Historical Society to maintain and operate the Cudahy Depot Museum of Cudahy History.

Note: Identifications read from left to right, front row to back.

CONTENTS

Cudahy's founder, Patrick Cudahy (March 17, 1849–July 29, 1919), is shown here seated at his business desk. The desk and chair can be seen at the Cudahy Historical Society Museum of Cudahy History at the Cudahy Depot. (Courtesy of Cudahy Historical Society.)

One

FORMATION

If Patrick Cudahy could see his city today, he would be pleased. When he bought land here, he envisioned a city growing around the meat packing plant he intended to build. He chose this location for the availability of water and the railroad, both of which were needed for his industry. The little settlement of Buckhorn—within the boundaries of his 700-acre purchase—boasted a railroad station named Buckhorn, a few farms, and four dirt roads. The Lake Road was an Indian trail along Lake Michigan; Kinnickinnic was another Indian trail along the railroad tracks; Chicago Road (now Whitnall Avenue) was an old Army road used to haul supplies between Chicago and Green Bay; and Packard Road was named after farmer Daniel Packard.

This was the scene in 1892 when construction was begun on the Cudahy Brothers Company building. Three other important events occurred during that year: an auction sold parcels of land for home and business development, and the Ponto Hotel and new railroad station were built. Renamed the Cudahy Depot, the new station replaced the old Buckhorn Station. The railroad was most significant to the growth of the settlement. It provided a means of shipping and receiving materials for the rapidly growing boomtown as well as transportation to the area.

With the basic needs of housing, employment, and transportation fulfilled, people flocked to the area, merchants followed, and so the little settlement grew into the Village of Cudahy in 1895. By 1906, the population increased sufficiently to qualify for incorporation as the City of Cudahy.

In 1892, an auction was held for the sale of land. People came from far and near to buy a lot in the new settlement. (Courtesy of Cudahy Public Library.)

Known as "Cudahy Cottages," these houses were built with high basements, where the owners lived until they could afford to build the rest of the house. Note the proud owner standing in front of his newly completed home. (Courtesy of Cudahy Public Library.)

The oldest house within the original City of Cudahy boundaries is located at 4527 South Packard Avenue. It was built by John Kiphutt in 1872, and sold in 1903 to Herman Mueller. It is commonly known as the Mueller home and still remains in the family. (Courtesy of Cudahy Public Library.)

The Columbia Hotel was located on the northwest corner of Packard and Plankinton Avenues. It was built to accommodate the traders who came to deal with Patrick Cudahy. It also housed a pool hall, grocery store, meeting hall, meat market, and barbershop. (Courtesy of Cudahy Public Library.)

The Theodore Ponto Hotel was under construction in 1892. It provided lodging for the construction workers building the new Cudahy meat packing plant and, later, for the workers employed there. The Cudahy Brothers Land Equipment Office is located next-door. The sign on front reads, "Call for plats' and prices." (Courtesy of Cudahy Public Library.)

The completed Ponto Hotel opened on Christmas Eve, 1893, on the northeast corner of Layton and Kinnickinnic Avenues. It had 16 sleeping rooms, a tavern, and a restaurant. The building still stands and is occupied by a tavern business. (Courtesy of Cudahy Public Library.)

There do not appear to be many spectators watching this parade as it marches south on Packard Avenue near Munkwitz Avenue. On the right is Glazier's Hall, a tavern and dance hall with picnic grounds at the rear. Note the hitching posts. (Courtesy of Cudahy Historical Society.)

This vehicle drew quite a bit of attention as it headed south near the corner of Packard and Layton Avenues in 1895. (Courtesy of Cudahy Historical Society.)

This horse and rig was traveling south on Packard Avenue just past the new Washington School and approaching the Falkowski Saloon and Behlendorf Grocery Store. Note the streetcar tracks on the unpaved road. (Courtesy of Cudahy Public Library.)

Packard Ave. looking South from Plankinton Ave., Cudahy, Wis.

This is a view of Packard Avenue looking south from Plankinton Avenue in the early 1900s. (Courtesy of Cudahy Historical Society.)

The intersection of Layton and Kingan Avenues is pictured here. Note the chicken picking in the dirt road. (Courtesy of Cudahy Historical Society.)

The Theodore Mahn orchard and farm on Lake Drive are pictured here. (Courtesy of Cudahy Historical Society.)

This is a view of a crew working at Pulaski Park from the site of the baseball diamond looking west in 1923. (Courtesy of Cudahy Historical Society.)

The wheelbarrows are all lined up for the crew working on the Mallory Avenue playground in 1923. (Courtesy of Cudahy Historical Society.)

This is a 1934 work project on Buckhorn Avenue looking north from Grange Avenue. (Courtesy of Cudahy Historical Society.)

Pictured here is the preparation for sidewalks on Grange Avenue, from Buckhorn Avenue looking west on Grange Avenue in 1934. (Courtesy of Cudahy Historical Society.)

In the early 1930s, the Civilian Conservation Corps built jetties and a road leading down the bluff to Lake Michigan in Sheridan Park. The buildings in the background are as follows: Red Star Yeast and Vinegar Works on the left, St. Ann's Orphanage summer home at center. The home was financed by Patrick Cudahy and named after his wife. (Courtesy of Cudahy Historical Society.)

Although not within city limits, the Milwaukee County Airport grew alongside the City of Cudahy. This is how it looked long before it became Mitchell International Airport. (Courtesy of Cudahy Historical Society.)

Office and yard crews pose at the Cudahy Depot. Built in 1892, a freight area was added in 1912. By 1971, shipping had declined, and the building was closed. In disrepair, it was condemned by the city and rescued by the Cudahy Historical Society who gained ownership in 1977 and restored it to its present state. (Courtesy of Cudahy Historical Society.)

A Chicago and Northwestern Railroad crew hitches a ride on a velocipede at the Cudahy Depot. Second from left is Tim O'Brien, Section Foreman, who came to Wisconsin to help lay double tracks between Chicago and Milwaukee. The others are unidentified. (Courtesy of Cudahy Public Library.)

This is a busy office staff at the Cudahy Depot in 1924. Pictured are Al Noderer, Fred Lambert, Sandy Jorgenseon, ? White, Eddie?, Alice (Stroinski) Jahn, and Otto Voigt. (Courtesy of Cudahy Historical Society.)

Fred H. Lambert began as a clerk at the Depot in 1908, and worked his way up to station agent in 1937. He is shown here at his desk in 1955, just two years before he retired. (Courtesy of Cudahy Historical Society.)

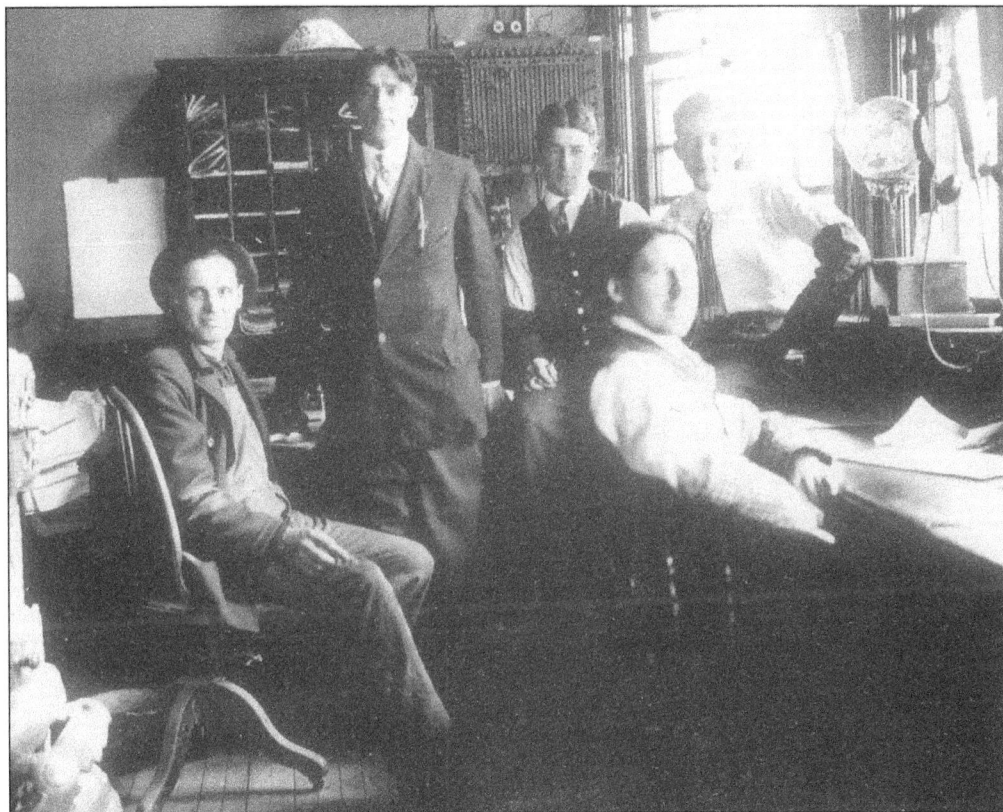

Pictured here is the inside of the dispatcher's room at the Cudahy Depot. (Courtesy of Cudahy Public Library.)

Fred. H. Lambert poses with a cartload of records written by him as an employee of the Chicago and Northwestern Railroad, 1928. (Courtesy of Cudahy Historical Society.)

Passengers are pictured boarding the train at the Cudahy Depot—a busy stop. Cudahy Brothers Company employees came to work and went home on a special train called "the scoot." Many immigrants from Europe arrived at the Depot to settle in Cudahy. During World War II, draftees boarded the train there en route to camp. Passenger service was discontinued in 1956. (Courtesy of Cudahy Public Library.)

Crowds line the tracks as the circus wagon train, en route from Baraboo to Milwaukee for the circus parade, makes a stop at the Cudahy Depot in 1992. (Courtesy of Cudahy Historical Society.)

Two

FOUNDATION

The first order of business for the fledgling city was forming a government. An election was held on April 3, 1906, choosing Dr. Arthur Sidler as the first Mayor. The city was divided into four wards with two aldermen elected from each. A new City Hall was built and city departments were established. The layout of streets and installation of sewers and water mains were major undertakings accomplished only by man and horsepower. With the groundwork laid, more businesses and industries arrived. Through Patrick Cudahy's foresight, separate residential, business, and industrial areas were designated.

The opening of Washington School in 1895 was the advent of Cudahy's present school system. Being the first, it was known only as "the school" until a second school named Lincoln was added in 1915.

The first three churches were built on land donated by Patrick Cudahy: St. Paul's Evangelical Lutheran in 1893, Cudahy Methodist in 1894, and St. Frederick Catholic in 1896. When he later desired the land for residential use, he traded the Methodist and Catholic Church lots for land on Plankinton Avenue and paid to move their buildings. This was typical procedure for the era. Records show that many buildings were moved to other locations. Relocations, business turnovers, and normal growth have greatly changed the face of the city over the generations.

The old City Hall was located on the 3600 block of Layton Avenue, east of the alley on the south side of the street. It housed the fire department, police department, jail, health department, city offices, council chambers, and—for a time—the library. Pictured in front are the firemen, with their horses and wagon. (Courtesy of the Cudahy Public Library.)

Dr. Arthur C. Sidler served as Mayor of the newly incorporated city from 1906 to 1908. (Courtesy of Cudahy Historical Society.)

Dr. Arthur C. Sidler is pictured here vacationing abroad in the early 1900s. (Courtesy of Cudahy Historical Society.)

City officials are pictured here in the council chambers at the old City Hall, 1928. Seated center are Edwin Gora, John Firer, John Schrank, and an unidentified woman. Seated at the desks are Art Schultz, William Lawler, Joseph Wagner, William Bunty, Frank Sobocinski, John Benka, Fred Schlueter Jr., and Harry Kennedy. (Courtesy of Cudahy Historical Society.)

City officials are pictured in the same room as above, 1956. The officials are Aldermen Neil Cory, Ernest Sadowski, Kieran Tobin, William Hoppe, Richard Little, Police Judge Gregory P. Gregory, City Clerk James Keller, Mayor Vincent Totka, City Attorney Milton Bedusek, Aldermen Frank Kluzinski, Frank Sobocinski, Michael Kovac, Rudy Palkowitz, Martin Mikula, and George Bong. (Courtesy of Cudahy Historical Society.)

The April 3, 1930 election resulted in a deadlock between John Benka, Inc. and Joseph Habanek for the 4th ward alderman position. Each received 293 votes. The two men agreed to pull straws for the position, and Habanek drew the lucky number. He is at the left and Mayor Charles Cassebaum is on the right. (Courtesy of Cudahy Historical Society.)

City Attorney Milton Bedusek, City Treasurer Steve Kowalowski, Mayor Vincent Totka, and City Clerk Kenneth Joslin are inspecting the new machine, which replaced the cigar box for collecting and posting city fees. A company representative demonstrates. (Courtesy of Cudahy Historical Society.)

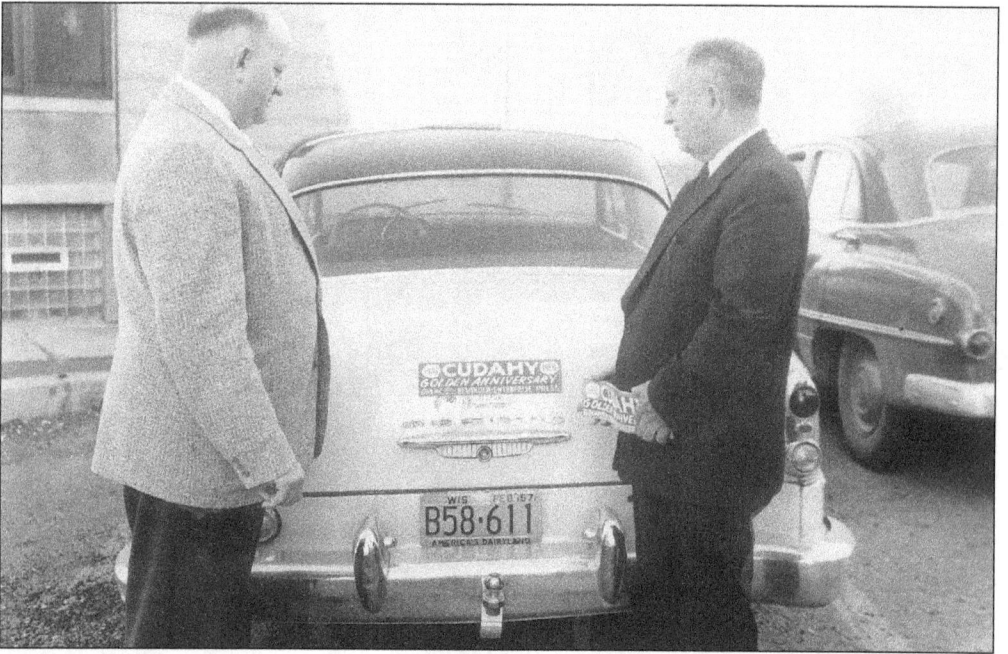

Alderman Michael Kovac and Mayor Vincent Totka approve a "Cudahy Golden Anniversary" bumper sticker in 1956. (Courtesy of Cudahy Historical Society.)

Looking over a mock-up of Packard Avenue are Mayor Vincent Totka, City Attorney Ed Minor, and a traffic safety officer. The Cudahy State Bank is under Mayor Totka's right hand. Across the street and northwest is Dettlaff's Drug Store, early 1940s. (Courtesy of Ken Joslin.)

26

Raising the first flag at the new City Hall on December 11, 1956, are Mayor Vincent Totka, Police Chief Anthony Wise, and City Engineer James Tiry. (Courtesy of Cudahy Historical Society.)

Observing the demolition of Red Star Yeast are Mayor Lawrence P. Kelly, City Clerk Frank Janicek, and Police Chief Anthony Wise. (Courtesy of Cudahy Historical Society.)

The wrecking ball strikes what is left of the old City Hall in January 1959. The new City Hall opened in 1956. (Courtesy of Cudahy Historical Society.)

The sidewalk superintendents, pictured here watching the razing of City Hall, were James Gaspardo, Melvin Weed, Walter Stock, and Louis Bedi. (Courtesy of Cudahy Historical Society.)

Only the skeleton remains of a once proud building. The restaurant at the left will also be razed to make room for the bank's drive-through and parking lot. (Courtesy of Cudahy Historical Society.)

Nothing is left but the foundation. (Courtesy of Cudahy Historical Society.)

This driver was ready for a fire in 1912—with his team of horses and hose, hook, and ladder wagon. The Cudahy Volunteer Fire Department organized in 1902, and was officially adopted by ordinance in 1908. (Courtesy of Cudahy Historical Society.)

The members of the Cudahy Volunteer Fire Department of 1914, pictured here, were (front row) Jerome Dretzka, Frank Jennejohn, William Fischer, Chief Fred Schlueter, John Jennejohn, Gerald Grebe, and Julius Seiy; (middle row) Vince Romanski, Herman Mueller, William Cassidy, Emil Noll, Mike Vasas, Mike Michalski, William Buntey, Art Markel, August Schlueter, Henry Sandel, and John Markel; (back row) John Thorne, John Medrow, John Schwartz, Walter Jopke, August Raasch, and Robert Medrow. (Courtesy of Cudahy Historical Society.)

Pictured here are members of the Cudahy Volunteer Fire Department with Chief Julius Seiy, c. 1920. Standing at far left is William Cassidy who died of head injuries suffered when he fell on ice while responding to a fire. (Courtesy of Cudahy Historical Society.)

Firefighters in gear stand by their engine in 1944. The men are (front row) Harry Slivinski, Al Ensslin, Ted Erdmann, Frank Spies, Vic Wachowski, Pat Behlendorf, Paul Danko, Fred Hecker, Hugo Littman, Jacob Spies, Charles Wolbert, and Chief Julius Seiy; (back row) Wallace Miller, William Marko, Charles Dronso, Al Brykczynski, Sam Belleranti, Art Wolbert, Sigmund Bukowski, Anton Seiy, and Robert Tice. (Courtesy of Cudahy Historical Society.)

Civilian Defense crews tested their water pumps at Sheridan Park pond in the early 1940s. (Courtesy of Ken Joslin.)

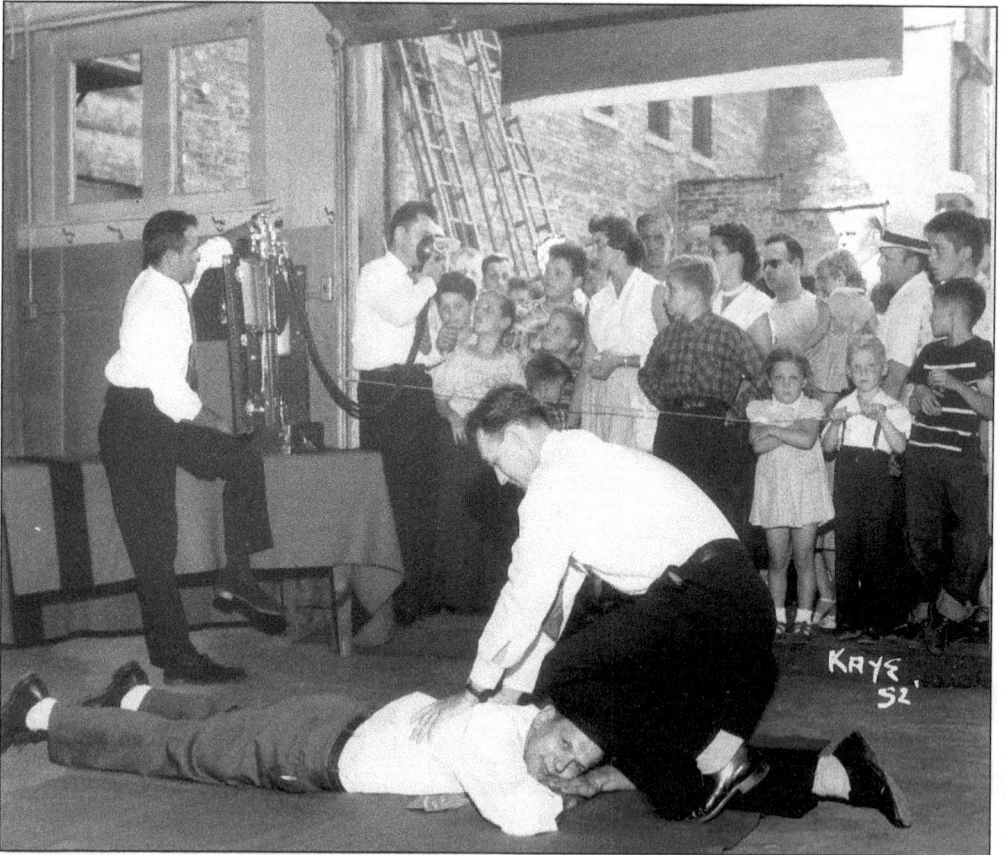

Joseph Marko, Eugene Milewski, John Kukor, and Vincent Slivinski are demonstrating artificial respiration to visitors at the fire department's golden anniversary open house in 1952. (Courtesy of Cudahy Historical Society.)

Firemen are seen here practicing their skills at a fire drill. (Courtesy of Cudahy Historical Society.)

The new fire station at 4624 South Packard Avenue is pictured here under construction in 1958. (Courtesy of Cudahy Historical Society.)

H.O. Krueger was the first Cudahy Police Chief from 1906 to 1914. Because there was not yet a Fire and Police Commission, he was appointed by the Common Council. (Courtesy of Cudahy Historical Society.)

The first jail and police department quarters faced the alley at the rear of the old City Hall. Built in 1908, it served the Department until 1956, when the new City Hall was built. (Courtesy of Cudahy Historical Society.)

Paul R. Littmann succeeded Krueger as Chief from 1914 to 1918. (Courtesy of Cudahy Historical Society.)

Police Chief John Medrow and Sgt. John Jurci examine a 1928 Chevy for damage in the old City Hall garage. (Courtesy of Cudahy Historical Society.)

Anthony M. Wise is sworn in as Police Chief by City Clerk James F. Keller in 1951. He went on to become the city's longest serving Chief and retired in 1987. (Courtesy of Cudahy Historical Society.)

This photo of the police department was taken in 1952, on the east side of the old City Hall. The policemen pictured here are (front row) Sgt. Robert Enbring, Detective Walter Sobocinski, Chief Anthony Wise, Sgt. John Jurci, and Sgt. Fred Schlueter; (back row) Patrolmen Peter Mizakowski, Daniel Kolosovsky, Charles Wolbert, Theodore Kramer, Rudy Zeman, Eugene Holubowicz, Andrew Masarik, John Wrazel, Milan Papala, Patrick Lathrop, and Steve Brinza. (Courtesy of Cudahy Historical Society.)

36

Chief Wise looks on as a teletype machine is installed at the new police headquarters in 1956. (Courtesy of Cudahy Historical Society.)

Police officers Pat Lathrop and Eric Plahna collaborate with these boy scouts on teaching safety during "Pedestrian Instruction Behavior Month" in June 1958. (Courtesy of Cudahy Historical Society.)

Police Chief Anthony Wise, City Electrician Joseph Zsebe, and Sgt. Patrick Lathrop adjust the timing for the intersection stoplights on the northwest corner of Layton and Packard Avenues in 1959. (Courtesy of Cudahy Historical Society.)

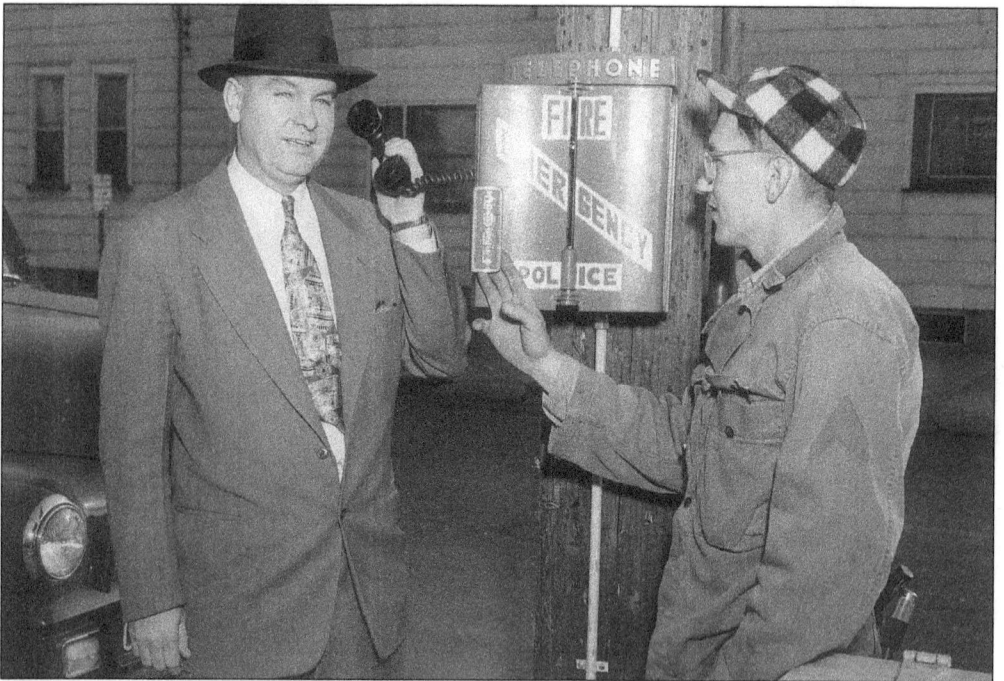

Chief Anthony Wise tests the new emergency call box. (Courtesy of Cudahy Historical Society.)

Donald Brzowski and Richard Shimeta shot two bull's-eyes at this bow and arrow target practice. Eugene Barcio watches. (Courtesy of Cudahy Historical Society.)

Donald Brzowski and Chief Anthony Wise observe shooters Steve Brinza, Rudy Zeman, Charles Wolbert, and Theodore Kramer at pistol target practice in City Hall's basement shooting range in 1962. (Courtesy of Cudahy Historical Society.)

Chief Wise shows off the new city ambulance to Sister Jean Winters and Sister Cleophas at Trinity Memorial Hospital in 1959. (Courtesy of Cudahy Historical Society.)

Sgt. Patrick Lathrop and Chief Wise commend Junior Police Officers in 1964. (Courtesy of Cudahy Historical Society.)

An applicant climbs a rope as part of the physical agility test for a police officer position in 1960. (Courtesy of Cudahy Historical Society.)

The Cudahy Police Department basketball team is suited up in 1966, for the annual charity game with the South Milwaukee Police. The players are (front row) Robert Maslowski, Thomas Putz, Joseph Kuban, Melvin Zemplinski, and Thomas Ciurlik; (back row) Gerald Witkowski, Roger Timm, and Gene Behnke. (Courtesy of Cudahy Historical Society.)

Horsepower was used to grade Packard Avenue, *c.* 1915. The first Lincoln School is in the background. (Courtesy of Cudahy Public Library.)

Sewer pipe is laid on Layton Avenue in front of the City Hall, *c.* 1906. (Courtesy of Cudahy Public Library.)

This is a view of more roadwork on Squire Avenue looking east from Kingan Avenue. (Courtesy of Cudahy Historical Society.)

The Rudolph Kerlin General Contractor's truck is blocking part of South Kingan Avenue at Armour Avenue looking north. The Vogl grocery store is at left. (Courtesy of Cudahy Historical Society.)

Mostly manpower was used to pave Packard Avenue between Plankinton and Layton Avenues in the early 1900s. (Courtesy of Cudahy Historical Society.)

This is a view of workers pouring cement on Packard Avenue one-half block north of Layton Avenue. (Courtesy of Cudahy Historical Society.)

Mayor Vincent Totka and city officials watch as the switch is pulled for new streetlights in the early 1950s. (Courtesy of Cudahy Historical Society.)

City crews spray trees to ward off Dutch Elm Disease in the 1950s. (Courtesy of Cudahy Historical Society.)

The Department of Public Works removes snow across the street from the Ladish Company after a big storm. (Courtesy of Cudahy Historical Society.)

Jim Senger, John Falkowski, and Norman Tichkowski are picking up Christmas trees. (Courtesy of Cudahy Historical Society.)

Garbage still needs to be collected in between snow removal. (Courtesy of Cudahy Historical Society.)

Peeking through a storm sewer are William Hoppe, Martin Mikula, Marv Lisowski, and Richard Hay. (Courtesy of Cudahy Historical Society.)

Marion E. Langdell was the first professional librarian hired by the city in 1948. Under her direction, the library was brought up to professional standards and the new memorial building was built. The city's first public library began at Frank's Drug Store in 1906. Subsequent moves were to the City Hall, to 3701 East Layton Avenue, to the Vocational School, and—finally—to its present building in 1952. (Courtesy of Cudahy Historical Society.)

Banners are waved as "Peacock Club" members celebrate at the end of the summer in 1952. The club was the Cudahy Public Library's summer reading program. (Courtesy of the Cudahy Public Library.)

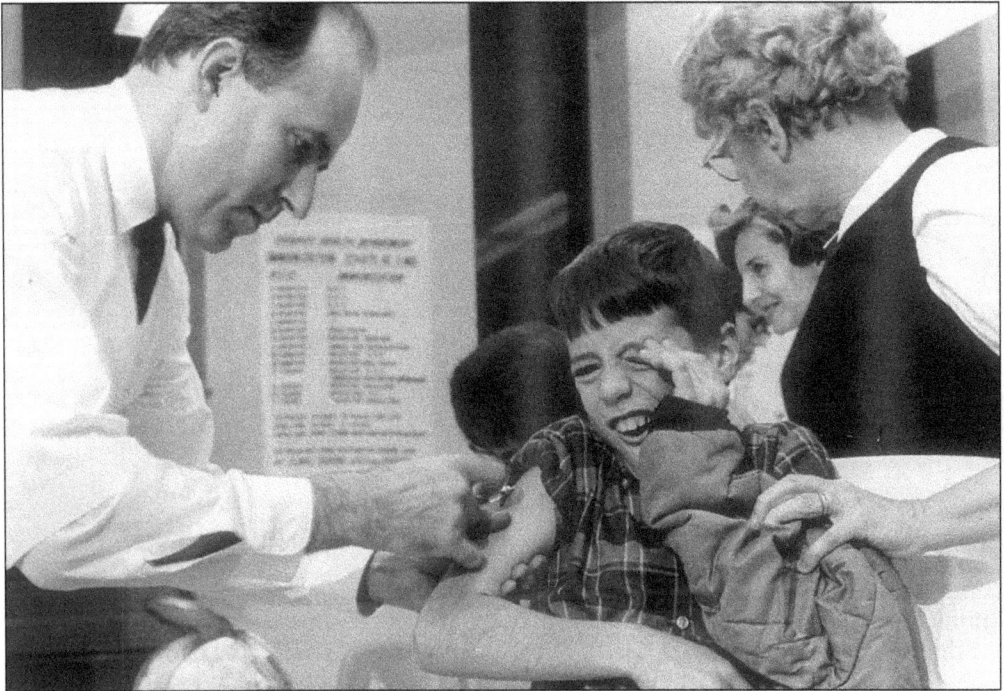

Dr. Carl Chelius, the Health Commissioner, administers a flu shot to Scott Urick, age nine, at the flu clinic at the Cudahy Health Department in 1967. (Courtesy of Cudahy Health Department.)

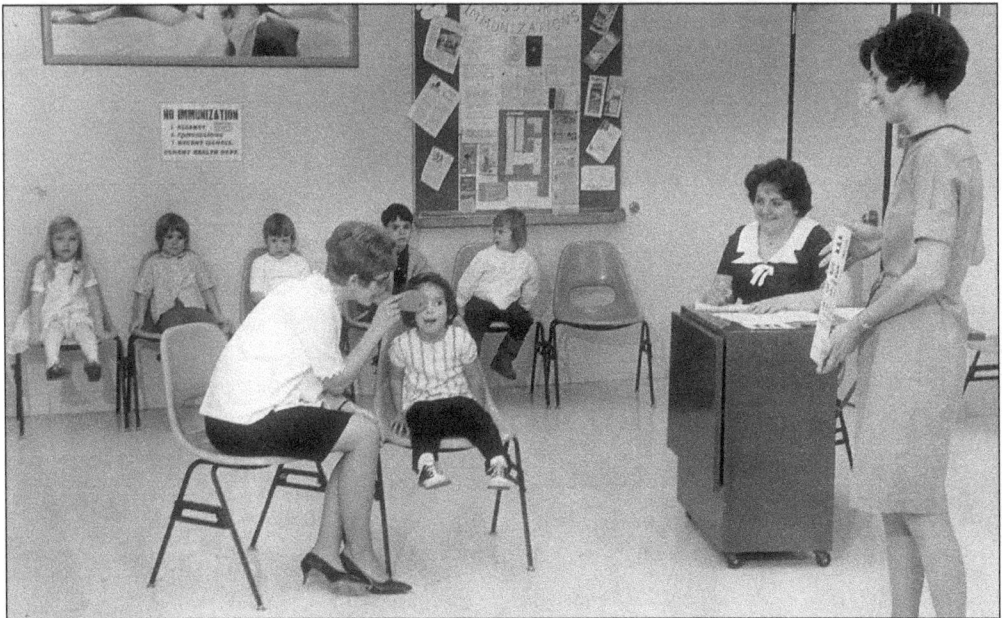

The Cudahy Jaycettes held a vision-screening clinic at the Cudahy Health Department on January 25, 1958. Pictured are Sue Rutledge examining Ellen Kresse, age three, Cindy Muszytowski, and Jean Kissling. The children in back are unidentified. (Courtesy of Cudahy Health Department.)

Trinity Memorial Hospital was under construction in 1956. A corporation was organized from the three communities of Cudahy, South Milwaukee, and Oak Creek for the purpose of building a hospital to serve the area. It was completed and opened its doors in May 1958. (Courtesy of St. Luke's South Shore Hospital (Formerly Trinity Memorial Hospital.)

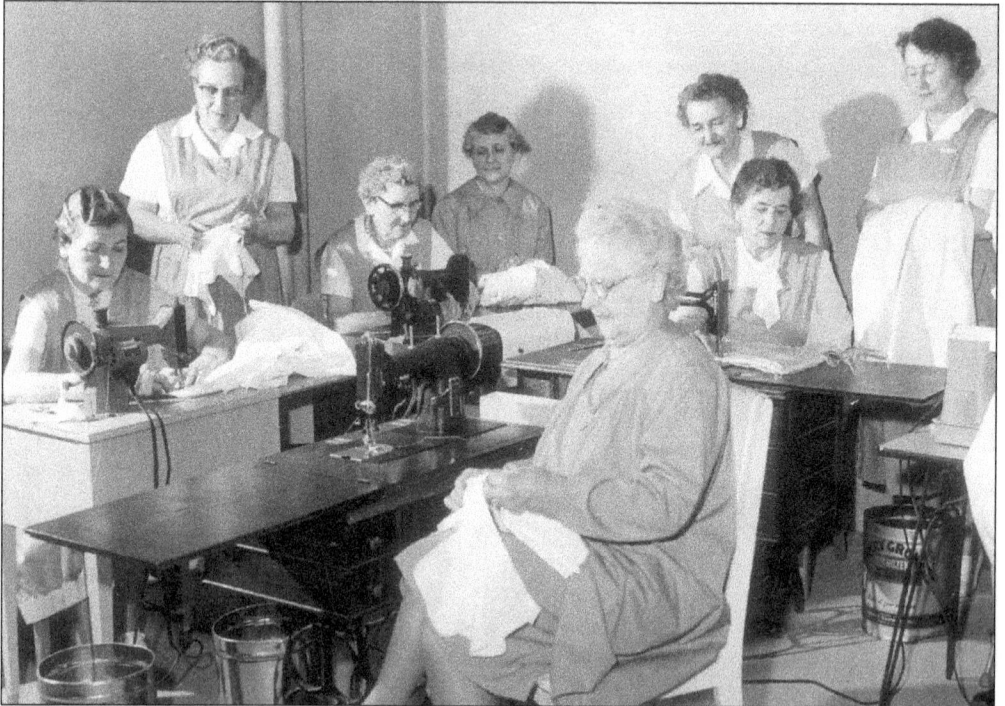

Trinity Memorial Hospital Auxiliary members are busy sewing robes and pajamas, and hemming bedding in preparation for the opening of the hospital. (Courtesy of St. Luke's South Shore Hospital (Formerly Trinity Memorial Hospital.)

This building is actually the second post office. It was located on the north side of the 3600 block of Layton Avenue just east of the alley. In later years, a second story was added and it became a tavern, which no longer stands. The first building was on Lipton Avenue between Plankinton and Layton Avenues. (Courtesy of Cudahy Historical Society.)

No weather conditions could keep these three postmen from delivering the mail. They are Fred Hoffman, Norman Harbrecht, and William Kohlhardt. (Courtesy of Cudahy Historical Society.)

Jesse F. Cory, the first Superintendent of Schools, is seated in his office at Washington School. (Courtesy of Cudahy Public Library.)

Cudahy teachers are pictured here in 1927. (Courtesy of Cudahy Historical Society.)

In 1962, the Kiwanis Club honored Cudahy teachers with 35 or more years of service. (Courtesy of Cudahy Historical Society.)

Washington School, the first school in the Village of Cudahy, was built in 1895. It stood on the east side of Packard Avenue between Barnard and Munkwitz Avenues. It served the city until declining enrollment forced it to close and be razed. (Courtesy of Cudahy Historical Society.)

A sixth grade class at Washington School is gathered here, c. 1923. Pictured are (first row) unidentified, Christy Becker, and three unidentified children; (second row) Elizabeth Serflek, Bernice Mack, Elizabeth Varsik, Pearl Kennedy, Margaret Petri, Mildred Snamiska, Catherine O'Dell, Ella Benedek, Kathryn Ferency, and Lena Tomaro; (third row) Mr. Bernard Hogue, teacher, Marshall Medrow, Terrence Jennejohn, and six unidentified children; (fourth row) Katherine Uher, Sylvia Klug, five unidentified children, Rebecca Frank, and Mary Pipis. (Courtesy of Cudahy Historical Society.)

This is the Washington School faculty, year unknown. The teachers are (front row) two unidentified, Angie Blair, Bess Waters, Helen Cavanaugh, and Rebecca Frank; (back row) Ellen Disch, Helen Getzin, Blanche Hayden, George Leider, Joseph Buichl, Kenneth Oudenhoven, Ray Mohr, unidentified, Ren Wright, and Ruth Howland. (Courtesy of Cudahy Historical Society.)

Discussing future plans with students are Anthony Bueckers, Dr. Joseph Kurtin, and George Dunn at Career Day in 1958. (Courtesy of Cudahy Historical Society.)

Vermetta Rapant, a crossing guard, and safety cadets leave for a trip to Washington D.C. in the mid 1960s. (Courtesy of Cudahy Historical Society.)

Lincoln School is pictured here shortly after it was built in 1915, on the east side of Packard Avenue between Allerton and Bottsford Avenues. For a period of time, it was also the junior high school. It served as an elementary school until it was demolished in 1991, and a new Lincoln School was built on its site. (Courtesy of Cudahy Public Library.)

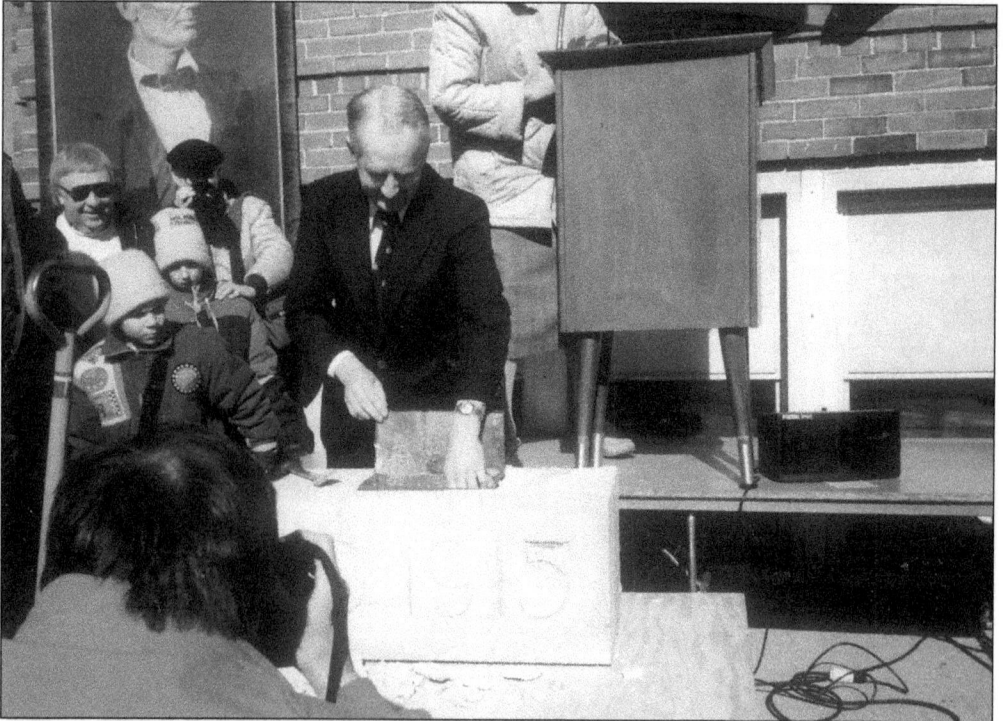

The cornerstone of the old building is opened by Principal Richard Jeffery at a ceremony sponsored by the Cudahy Historical Society on February 2, 1991. At left in sunglasses is John Watson, the Superintendent of Schools. (Courtesy of Cudahy Historical Society.)

Pictured here is part of the crowd at the cornerstone opening on February 2, 1991. (Courtesy of Cudahy Historical Society.)

The Lincoln School was demolished in February 1991. Another old building falls to the wrecking ball. (Courtesy of Cudahy Historical Society.)

The new Lincoln School is pictured here as it looked under construction in 1991. (Courtesy of Cudahy Historical Society.)

Miss Alfreda Holman poses with her class outside the new high school, c. 1930. (Courtesy of Cudahy Historical Society.)

The Cudahy High School Band and Director Oscar Kluck pose at Lincoln School in 1926, before the move to the new high school. (Courtesy of Cudahy Historical Society.)

Cudahy High School, located on the west side of Lake Drive between Munkwitz and Somers Avenues, was built in 1926. Additions were built for a gymnasium and pool in 1929, and a study hall, library, and cafeteria were added in 1939. In 1965, a new high school was opened across the street. The old building was used as a junior high and later as a second high school campus until it was razed in 1992. (Courtesy of Cudahy Historical Society.)

Principal Bernard Hogue at far right was advisor to the Radio Club at Cudahy High School in the 1940s. (Courtesy of Cudahy Historical Society.)

The Holman sisters, Marie and Alfreda, were longtime teachers in the Cudahy school system. They are pictured here working at a bake sale fundraiser. (Courtesy of Cudahy Historical Society.)

A group of Cudahy High School students pose before leaving on a trip to Washington D.C. and New York City. They are chaperoned by Mr. And Mrs. Victor Liska (front row left) and Barbara and Fred Wetzel (second row left). (Courtesy of Cudahy Historical Society.)

Cudahy High School sports teams have always attracted community interest. Pictured here is the 1965 football team coached by Nick Milinovich, standing at far left, and Joe Kukor, standing at far right. (Courtesy of Cudahy Historical Society.)

Rooting for their team are the 1968-69 cheerleaders. They are (front row) Debbie Barth, Judy Furdek, Pat Linde, and Susan Schmitz; (back row) Lynn Lewandowski, Catherine Bobrowicz, Sue Schroettner, and Wendy Gretz. (Courtesy of Cudahy Historical Society.)

Mrs. Louis Pillsbury, representing the family of General Billy Mitchell, presents a plaque in his honor to John Wohlfarth, Principal of Mitchell School, at its dedication ceremony on December 8, 1968. (Courtesy of George Slupski, Principal, General Mitchell School.)

These students in costume are on stage and ready to take part in an operetta at Kosciuszko School in 1928. Located at 5252 South Kirkwood Avenue, the school was built in 1922, to accommodate the fast-growing population on the south side of the city. It was closed in the late 1980s and reopened for classes in the 1990s. (Courtesy of Cudahy Historical Society.)

Police Officer Dan Kolosovsky, Principal Floyd Rabehl, and Ozzie the Clown conduct a safety program at Kosciuszko School in 1964. (Courtesy of Cudahy Historical Society.)

Costumes of all kinds can be seen in this picture of the fifth grade class at the J.E. Jones School's Halloween party in 1962. (Courtesy of Cudahy Historical Society.)

Holy Family School was built on the corner of Swift and Hammond Avenues in 1910. It had four classrooms, a parish hall, and living quarters for the nuns. By 1924, the congregation tripled, and the hall was converted to four more classrooms. In 1958, a new school was built at the site. (Courtesy of the Archdiocese of Milwaukee Archives.)

Teacher Frank Garstecki and the Holy Family graduation class of 1910 pose for a photograph. (Courtesy of Cudahy Historical Society.)

The Cudahy Vocational School building on Swift and Squire Avenues was built in 1927. Prior to that, classes were held in another facility. From 1940 to 1952, the library was also housed in the building. (Courtesy of Cudahy Historical Society.)

A handshake seals the deal for an addition to the Vocational School in 1938. Pictured here are "Shorty" Sztukowski, James Keller, Chris F. Becker, Mayor Charles Cassebaum, and Vocational School Director Robert L. Gruber. (Courtesy of Cudahy Historical Society.)

Work begins on the addition at this groundbreaking ceremony in 1938. (Courtesy of Cudahy Historical Society.)

The home economics addition to the school was completed in 1938. It faced Squire Avenue just East of Swift Avenue. (Courtesy of Cudahy Historical Society.)

Trying on hats made by the millinery class at a 1952 Cudahy Vocational School open house are Marion (Strehlow) Marino, Theresa Seiy, Linda Schattschneider, Joan (Seiy) Paul, and Nancy Coffenburg. (Courtesy of Cudahy Historical Society.)

Students model fashions made in sewing class at Vocational School at an outdoor-style show in 1962. (Courtesy of Cudahy Historical Society.)

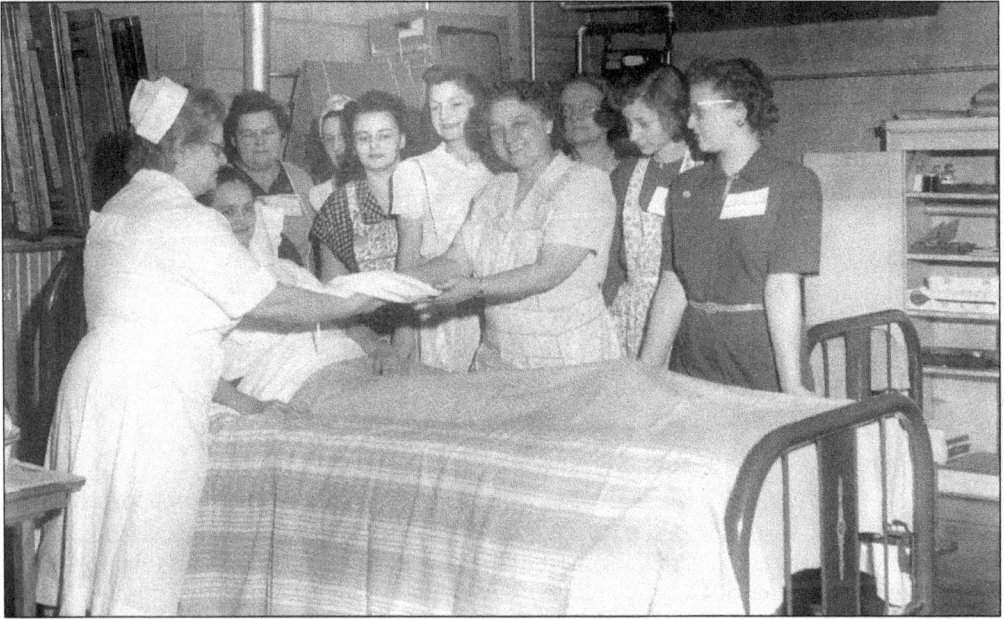

A home-nursing class at Cudahy Vocational School poses in the early 1950s. The nurse is unidentified, and the patient is Dorothy Doe. The students are Helen Magnus, Jean Leavitt, Esther Snamiska, two unidentified women, Dorothy Brostowicz, and Elinor Plahna. (Courtesy of Cudahy Historical Society.)

Cudahy public school teachers attend a class in civilian defense at the Vocational School in the 1960s. (Courtesy of Cudahy Historical Society.)

A group of students at St. Paul's Evangelical Lutheran Church are pictured here. Built in 1893, at the southwest corner of Cudahy and Swift Avenues on land donated by Patrick Cudahy, it is the oldest church in Cudahy. The parsonage is at the right. (Courtesy of the Cudahy Public Library)

Parishioners stand proudly outside of the new St. Frederick Catholic Church built in 1896 at the southeast corner of Cudahy and Swift Avenues, across the street and east of St. Paul's, on land donated by Patrick Cudahy. The building was moved three times: first, to the east, where school rooms were added; second, to Plankinton Avenue; and third, to 3866 East Layton Avenue, where it became a place of business. It still stands there today. (Courtesy of St. Frederick Catholic Church.)

Land was purchased and construction began on the first St. Joseph's Church in 1908. It was built to meet the needs of the Czechoslovakian community in Cudahy. (Courtesy of Cudahy Historical Society.)

The interior of the first St. Joseph's Church is pictured here. (Courtesy of Cudahy Historical Society.)

The Cudahy Evangelical Lutheran Church at 3515 East Van Norman Avenue was completed in 1929. In 1956, when a new building was planned for the site, it was moved to Pennsylvania Avenue where it became the Little Tigers Soccer Clubhouse and is now the Southwoods Restaurant. (Courtesy of Cudahy Historical Society.)

A new church with a new name—St. Mark's Evangelical Lutheran Church replaced the Cudahy Evangelical Lutheran Church. (Courtesy of Cudahy Historical Society.)

St. John's Evangelical Lutheran Church is pictured here as it looked when completed in 1962. Parsonage and child day care wings were added later. (Courtesy of Cudahy Historical Society.)

Admiring the new church directory sign on Lake Drive and College Avenue are "Support of Churches Committee" members Jordan Puetz, the builder of the sign; Henry Ryczek; Frank Taucher; Rev. George Kolanda; and Rev. Donald Surgess. (Courtesy of Cudahy Historical Society.)

The first Holy Family Church was built in 1901, on land donated by Michael Cudahy Sr. The congregation formed in 1900, to perpetuate their Polish heritage. The present church building, on the same site at 3767 East Underwood Avenue, was dedicated in June 1931. (Courtesy of the Archdiocese of Milwaukee Archives.)

The Cudahy Methodist Church, founded in 1888, built its first church in 1894, on Swift Avenue between Armour and Van Norman Avenues. That same building is pictured here after it was moved to Plankinton Avenue. The congregation occupied it until 1963, when a new church was built at 5865 South Lake Drive. (Courtesy of Della Essig, Cudahy United Methodist Church.)

This is the inside the John W. Strandt Funeral Home at 716 (3600) East Layton Avenue in the early 1900s. (Courtesy of Cudahy Historical Society.)

Patients, a nurse, and Dr. Arthur Sidler—the first Mayor of Cudahy—gather in his upstairs office on the northeast corner of Packard and Barnard Avenues in 1910. (Courtesy of Cudahy Historical Society.)

The Freudenberg Bakery, the first bakery in the city, is pictured as it looked in 1898. The building still stands at 3813 East Barnard Avenue. Pictured here are Hanna Christiana Winkler Freudenberg (Fritz's mother), Christina Breuer Freudenberg, and Johann Friedrich (Fritz) Freudenberg. (Courtesy of Cudahy Historical Society.)

This is the Cudahy Fuel Company yard and office at 5009 South Packard Avenue in 1922. Christ F. Becker is at left, and Hilbert Becker is at far right. (Courtesy of Cudahy Historical Society.)

This tavern owned by Albert August Sr. and August Stressing Jr., was originally located at 3383 East Layton Avenue. It was moved to the northwest corner of Packard and Layton Avenues when it was owned by Fred Schlueter. It later became the Dettlaff Drug Store, and now is the site of the M & I Bank. (Courtesy of Cudahy Public Library.)

Two hunters admire their day's hunt in front of the Gust Schienbein tavern at 3361 East Layton Avenue, *c.* 1900. (Courtesy of Cudahy Public Library.)

Family members pose outside Nessler's Restaurant at 3534 East Layton Avenue. The sign on the window advertises ice cream. It was the early 1900s. The building still stands today. (Courtesy of Cudahy Public Library.)

Local patrons hoist their drinks while bartenders Steve and Mary Sevela look on. The year was 1934, according to the calendar on the wall. (Courtesy of Cudahy Historical Society.)

Joe Venus operated the first bowling alley in the city. (Courtesy of Cudahy Public Library.)

This tavern at 3479 East Plankinton Avenue has had several owners. Christ Woehsner owned it at the time this picture was taken, c. 1915. Bowling alleys were installed and later removed. A barbershop run by Louis Csepella was also housed in the building. (Courtesy of Cudahy Historical Society.)

This is the original Cudahy State Bank built in 1909, at 4753 South Packard Avenue. It later became Magyera's Paint & Art Store and—most recently—the Greek Island Restaurant. (Courtesy of Cudahy Public Library.)

The Cudahy State Bank built a new building in 1919, at 4702 South Packard Avenue. The four-sided clock was a landmark on Packard Avenue. The bank joined the Marine Corporation in the 1960s and now is Bank One. (Courtesy of Cudahy Historical Society.)

This is the interior of the Cudahy State Bank at its grand opening in 1919. (Courtesy of Cudahy Historical Society.)

The 25th anniversary of Dretzka's Department Store was celebrated by this group of people in 1926. Mr. and Mrs. Frank Dretzka are 6th and 7th from left in the second row. (Courtesy of Cudahy Historical Society.)

Banners in the windows advertise another Dretzka's anniversary, celebrated with a sale. (Courtesy of Cudahy Historical Society.)

This is the interior of the Cudahy Flour & Feed Company at 3630 East Munkwitz Avenue. The Company handled seeds of all kinds, flour, sugar, chicken feed, eggs, straw, hay, and fertilizer. Pictured are Pater Benka, Joe Kujawa, and an unidentified man. (Courtesy of Cudahy Historical Society.)

Peter Benka and an unidentified person stand outside the Cudahy Flour & Feed Company, c. 1930. The sign in the window says "Sensational Offer! Get this beautiful table lamp valued at $7.99 for only $1.98 with 2 Schlitz malt labels." (Courtesy of Cudahy Historical Society.)

This is the inside of the Behlendorf Grocery Store on Packard Avenue in the early 1900s. Note the hanging kerosene lamp and display of tomato soup at 10¢ a can. (Courtesy of Cudahy Public Library.)

Anton Adamczyk is pictured here inside his grocery and meat market on Hammond Avenue in 1938. The store, an institution on Cudahy's south side, is still operated by family members. (Courtesy of Cudahy Historical Society.)

Bronislaw Holubowicz stands behind the counter of the grocery store he ran with his wife Serafina at 3677 East Squire Avenue from 1918 to 1955. This picture was taken in the early 1940s. There is an OPA regulation sign above the cash register and a "War Bond" poster to the right of it. (Courtesy of Cudahy Historical Society.)

A City of Cudahy truck "gasses up" at Ed & Erv's Texaco Station, 5003 South Packard Avenue, in the 1950s. (Courtesy of Cudahy Historical Society.)

Cy and Carl Hepp ran the Master Motors Service at 3540 East Layton Avenue. Cy is at the far right next to the gas pump in this picture from the late 1930s. The others are unidentified. Signs advertise Moco batteries and Atlas tires. (Courtesy of Donna Hepp Burak and Carl Hepp.)

Three gas pumps and three attendants are ready to provide service at the Koehler Service Station at 3503 East Layton Avenue in 1946. (Courtesy of Cudahy Historical Society.)

Fred Olson, employee of Tomaro Contractors, Inc., poses with a Bucyrus Erie hydro crane in the 1950s. Tomaro Contractors did much of the sewer and water installation and concrete work in the early days of the city. (Courtesy of Cudahy Historical Society.)

Venus Motor Sales featured Mobil gas at their pumps at 5002 South Packard Avenue, c. 1939. A tire pump is at the left. Note the streetcar tracks on Packard Avenue. (Courtesy of Cudahy Historical Society.)

A crowd gathers while Mayor Cornelius Ames shakes hands with the Phillip Morris Kid outside Sullivan's Shoe Shine Parlor at 4714 South Packard Avenue, c. 1937. Watching are Tommy Sullivan, Police Chief John Medrow, Alderman Gerald Walsh, City Clerk James Keller, and Police Judge Floyd Gonyea. (Courtesy of Cudahy Historical Society.)

Children are treated to a special "Hopalong Cassidy Savings Club and Rodeo" at the Majestic Theater. The bank officers present are Walter Stock, C. Harold Nicolaus, and Melvin Weed (at far right). (Courtesy of Cudahy Historical Society.)

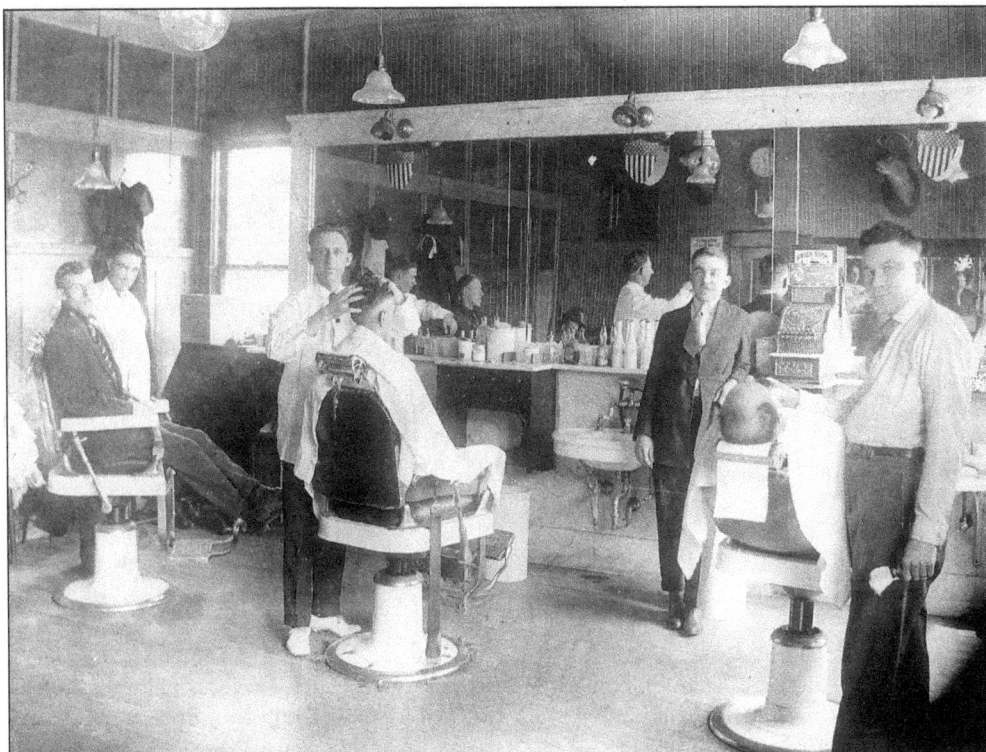

This is the inside of Horner's Barber Shop at 3460 East Layton Avenue in 1918. Note the center hair part on the barber at left and the "above-the-ears" cut on youngster at center. (Courtesy of Cudahy Historical Society.)

Cudahy Lumber & Supply Corporation was in business from 1922 to 1981. This picture was taken in the late 1930s. The building still stands at 5334 South Packard Avenue. (Courtesy of Cudahy Historical Society.)

The Sheridan Hotel, a Cudahy landmark located at 5133 S. Lake Drive, is pictured here as it looked in the 1920s. The sign at the curb reads as follows: "Stop Motorists at the Hotel Sheridan." (Courtesy of Cudahy Historical Society.)

Gora's Pharmacy at 3779 East Pulaski Avenue offered more than drugs for sale. Owner Edwin Gora advertised soda, grill, and Wisconsin ice cream. (Courtesy of Cudahy Historical Society.)

This is Pulaski Hall and Tavern. "Hall For Rent For All Occasions," reads the sign. The building has been remodeled since this picture was taken in 1956. It was operated by the Glowacki family for many years. (Courtesy of Mary Glowacki.)

Sears celebrated its "diamond jubilee" with a huge cake at its Packard Plaza store in 1961. In this photograph, Mayor Vincent Totka has the honor of cutting the cake. (Courtesy of Cudahy Historical Society.)

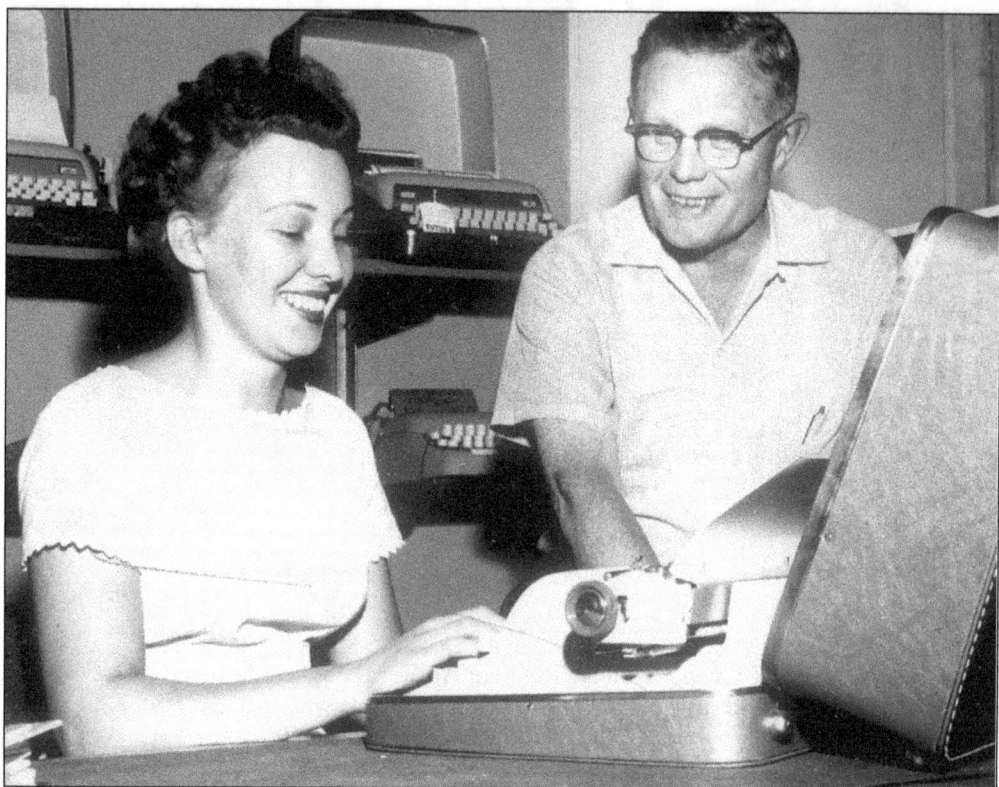

Donald Murphy, owner of D & E Office Supplies, looks on as Joan Scianni wins the typing contest sponsored by the store at this Sidewalk Bazaar in 1961. (Courtesy of Cudahy Historical Society.)

Charlotte Bird is chosen as "Miss Cudahy" in the late 1940s. Claude Robarge of Cudahy Brothers Company is at left, and Mayor Vincent Totka is at right. Note the peacock feathers in the background. (Courtesy of Ken Joslin.)

The cornerstone of the Cudahy Brothers Company plant was laid on August 15, 1892. The building was completed on schedule on November1, 1893. (Courtesy of Cudahy Historical Society.)

This is the hog-kill department at the Cudahy Brothers Company in the early 1920s. (Courtesy of Cudahy Historical Society.)

Employees of the lard department take a break with their products: Cudahy Brothers Company Lard, Cudahy's Milwaukee SnowBall, Cudahy's Milwaukee White Champion, Leaf Lard, Queen's Brand Pure Refined Lard, and Special Pure Lard. (Courtesy of Cudahy Historical Society.)

This is a peek inside the Company Store in 1923. (Courtesy of Cudahy Historical Society.)

The purpose of this meeting is unknown. It is possibly a rehearsal of the Peacock Quartet, with the accompanist seated at the piano. (Courtesy of Cudahy Historical Society.)

Cudahy was known as the "Peacock City," after the Peacock line of meats advertised on this barn. (Courtesy of Cudahy Historical Society.)

Cudahy Brothers Company Works Council company representatives are pictured here in 1921. (Courtesy of Cudahy Historical Society.)

The actor Thomas Mitchell was featured in a weekly television series, sponsored by Patrick Cudahy, Inc. in the 1950s. He was given a company tour by Henry Adlam (at left) when this picture was taken. (Courtesy of Cudahy Historical Society.)

City officials are celebrating "National Hot Dog Month" at the City Hall in 1957. Seated are William Hoppe, Ernest Sadowski, Kenneth Joslin, Mayor Vincent Totka, Dorothy Ladwig, Michael Kovac, Rudolph Palkowicz, and Niel Cory. Standing are James Tiry, Fred Schlueter, Stephen Kowalowski, Herman Steffen, Sigmund Bukowski, Anthony Wise, Theodore Kramer, Frank Sobocinski, Frank Kluzinski, and George Bong. (Courtesy of Cudahy Historical Society.)

This picture from 1910 shows Ladish's future land site. Note the three companies already existing: Geo. J. Meyer Company, Federal Rubber Company, and Cudahy Brothers Company. (Courtesy of Cudahy Historical Society.)

Ladish Drop Forge Company is pictured here as it looked in 1917. The company began as Obenberger Drop Forge Company. It moved to Cudahy in 1912, helped by a loan from Patrick Cudahy. (Courtesy of Cudahy Historical Society.)

This is the Ladish Drop Forge Company forge shop in 1938. Pictured is a single action hammer in the open frame department in a drawing operation. Three men are required to handle the tongs to move it into position. (Courtesy of Cudahy Historical Society.)

This picture shows the destruction caused by the million-dollar fire that devastated the Ladish metallurgical department in 1948. Fortunately there was no loss of life. Department employees remembered the gritty, painstaking recovery and restoration of irreplaceable test reports, forms, and records. (Courtesy of Cudahy Historical Society.)

Owner and founding father Herman Ladish meets with the Board of Directors in 1958 to christen the #85 hammer. Mr. Ladish is fifth from the left. (Courtesy of Cudahy Historical Society.)

This is the Federal Rubber Company in the early 1900s. (Courtesy of Cudahy Historical Society.)

Foremen dressed in their Sunday best pose outside the Federal Rubber Company in 1910. (Courtesy of Cudahy Historical Society.)

Girls from the Federal Rubber Company trimming department pose for this picture in 1912. (Courtesy of Cudahy Historical Society.)

People enjoy an outing from Federal Rubber Company, post 1917. The banner on the car advertises "Milwaukee (unknown) Cycle Club Run," possibly a bicycle race. (Courtesy of Cudahy Historical Society.)

Pepsi Cola Company of Detroit, Michigan, is loading a shipment of bottling equipment from Geo. J. Meyer Manufacturing Company on March 28, 1960. (Courtesy of Cudahy Historical Society.)

Jan Bader, Service Engineer at Geo. J. Meyer Manufacturing Company, shows off the Meyer electronic inspecting machine. (Courtesy of Cudahy Historical Society.)

This is a view of the Meyer Company building, facing Kingan Avenue, in the 1980s before it was razed. (Courtesy of Cudahy Historical Society.)

Red Star Yeast was established in 1882 along the lakefront. Its products were yeast and vinegar. The company suffered major fires in 1958, and again in 1959. It was razed later that year. (Courtesy of Cudahy Historical Society.)

Three

FUN

L ife in Cudahy was not all work and no play. People found many ways to entertain themselves. Clubs were formed, many centering at the churches; others were formed purely as social or service organizations.

Staging dramas was a favorite pastime. Plays were held at the Kleineider Hall on Packard Avenue and at the various church halls. They provided entertainment not only for the audience but for the participants as well. For those not so inclined, the motion picture theaters afforded another form of fun.

Cudahy can boast of parkland on its eastern boundary all the way from the northern to the southern city limits. Sheridan Park was built on the lakefront on land sold at a fair price by Patrick Cudahy. Pulaski, Warnimont, and Cudahy Parks were added later. The parks offered many recreational opportunities.

Cudahy has long been a sports-oriented city and has enthusiastically supported its teams. Individual sports were also popular, and performing arts were prevalent. Hometown musical talent enlivened many celebrations and parades. The following pictures show the diversity of leisure time activities enjoyed by all.

This baseball team picture was taken on Barnard Avenue in the early 1900s. In the background at far left is Washington School. Across the street facing Packard Avenue is the Evangelical Christus Church, which was later moved around the corner to face Barnard Avenue. (Courtesy of Cudahy Historical Society.)

This is the "Cudahy Special" baseball team in 1907. Robert Medrow is top right. Joseph Wagner, who served as Mayor from 1932 to 1936, is front right. The others are unidentified. (Courtesy of Cudahy Historical Society.)

The banner says it all for this championship Cudahy Legion team in 1930. (Courtesy of Cudahy Historical Society.)

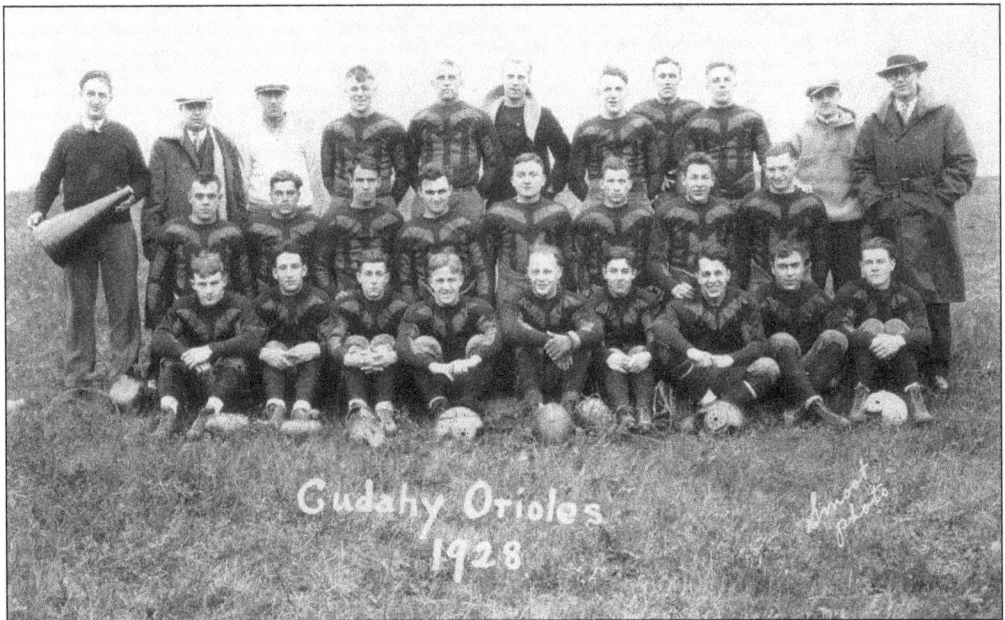

The Cudahy Orioles football team played at Sheridan Park south of the lagoon. The players also marked the field. There were no bleachers, so fans stood and watched the games. (Courtesy of Cudahy Historical Society.)

Cudahy High School basketball team and coach pose for this photograph in 1923. (Courtesy of Cudahy Historical Society.)

This is the Cudahy Junior High School 8th grade championship basketball team of 1927. The team members are (front row) Carl Jarosek, John Janto, Eloise Wilson, Peter Delson, and Stanley Voight; (back row) Clarence Burns, John Nemeth, an unidentified player, Walter Schuetz, Fritz Greinke, and another unidentified player. (Courtesy of Cudahy Historical Society.)

Members of the 1925 Cudahy High School girl's basketball team gather around their trophy for a photograph. (Courtesy of Cudahy Historical Society.)

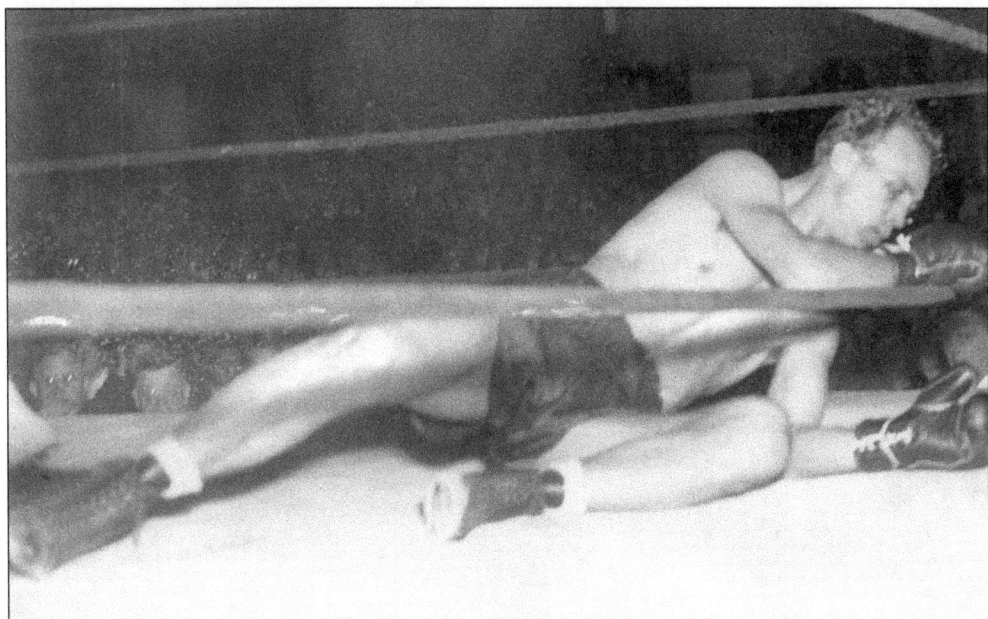

Cudahy lightweight boxer Tait Littman is down for the count. (Courtesy of Cudahy Historical Society.)

The Germania Society enacts a mock wedding in the late 1920s. The society members are (front row) Freida Jennejohn, Millie Peterson, an unidentified person, and Frances Young; (back row) Katherine Hinger, Ann Strehlow, two unidentified people, Augusta Medrow, Tillie Sobieszak, Emma Chapman, Ida Jennejohn, Martha Ollmann, and Mathilda Kimnach. (Courtesy of Cudahy Historical Society.)

The Knights of Pythias Lodge celebrate Halloween at Kleineider's Hall, *c.* 1920. (Courtesy of Cudahy Historical Society.)

Jesse F. Cory, the Superintendent of Schools and Scout Commissioner, received this picture from the boy scouts of Troop 60 in 1918. (Courtesy of Cudahy Historical Society.)

The Junior Chamber of Commerce received its charter award at a banquet in 1938. Of special note is Milwaukee Mayor Carl Zeidler on the left. The others are Jaycee President J. R. Meyers, the Milwaukee area Jaycee President, and George Dunn. (Courtesy of Cudahy Historical Society.)

The Cudahy Municipal Legion Band poses for a photograph at the 1928 Wisconsin State Fair. (Courtesy of Cudahy Historical Society.)

Getting out the *Tracer* newspaper to Cudahy servicemen during World War II are members of the Cudahy Jaycees and the Cudahy Service League. Pictured are (seated) Elizabeth Kudlovics, Clara Snamiska, and Rose Steffen; (standing) John Varsik, Edith Schmidt, Doris Angelroth, and Rev. Paul Valentiner. (Courtesy of Cudahy Historical Society.)

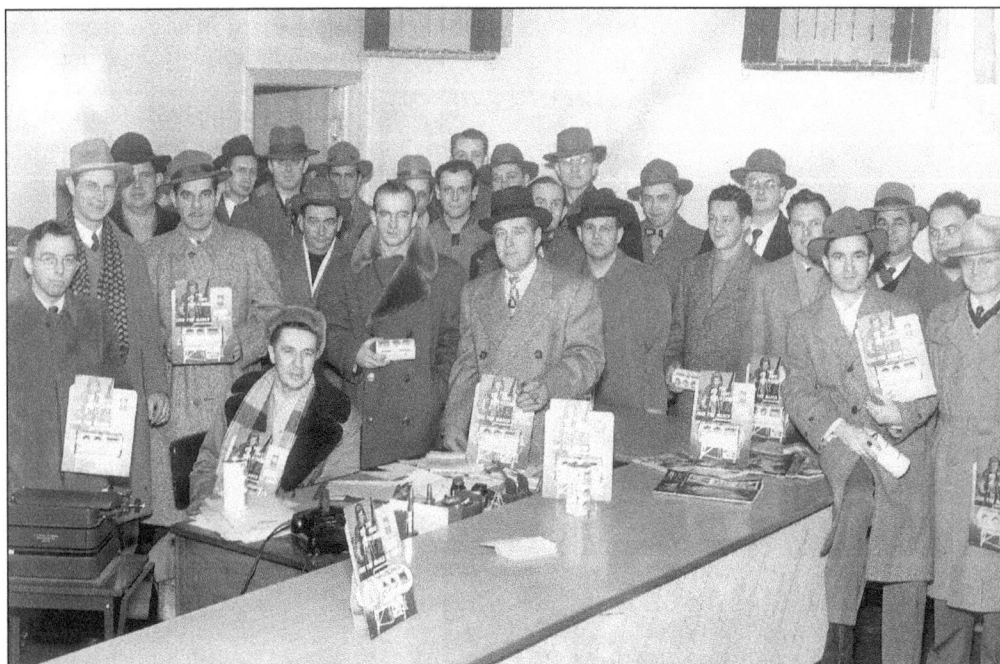

Ready to begin a door-to-door campaign for the March of Dimes are the Cudahy Jaycees, late 1940s. Seated at the desk in his office is Hubert Dretzka. (Courtesy of Cudahy Historical Society.)

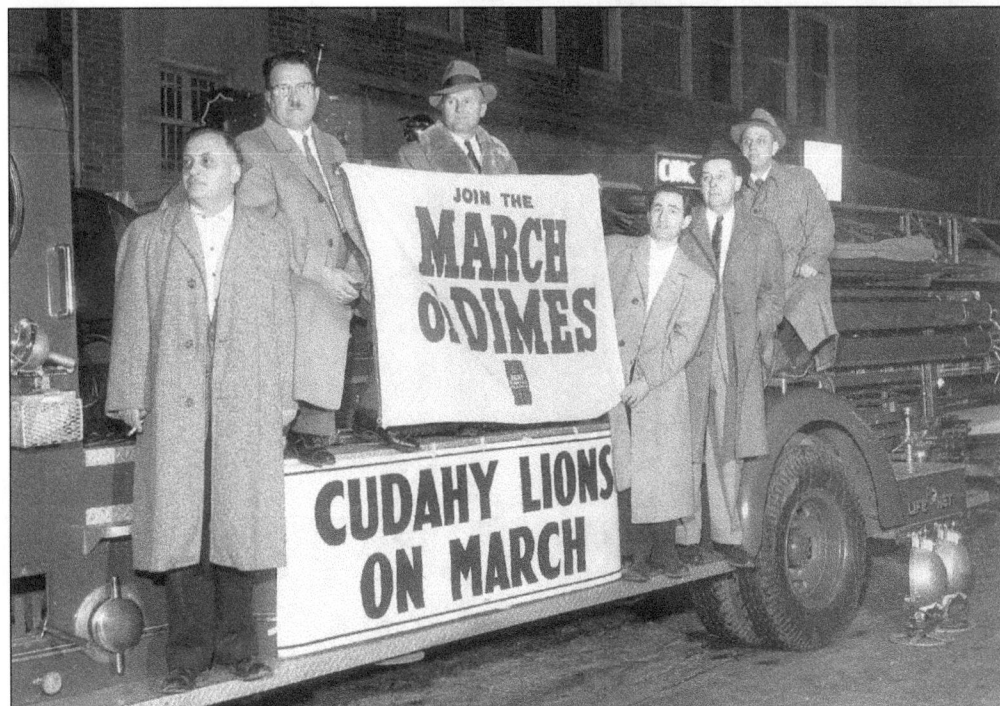

The Lions Club took over for the Jaycees and sponsored the March of Dimes campaign in the 1950s. Pictured here are Wally Nero, Joseph Kujawa, Sigmund Bukowski, Ralph Logan, Lawrence Kelly, and Frank Drucas. (Courtesy of Cudahy Historical Society)

The Cudahy Historical Society sold a commemorative plate depicting landmarks of the city for the city's 75th anniversary in 1981. Pictured are Priscilla Schroettner and Lydia Zaborski. (Courtesy of Cudahy Historical Society.)

Dr. Edward Tomasik is handing over the gavel to Gerald Ponec at a meeting of the Polish National Alliance. The ladies are Joyce Parker, Dolores Kanyuh, and Dolores Tomasik. (Courtesy of Cudahy Historical Society.)

Beatrice Nevshemal hands over the reigns as president of the Auxiliary of VFW Chapter 2895 to her daughter Juan Lohr in 1951. John Kalman on the right succeeded John Janto as Post Commander. (Courtesy of Cudahy Historical Society.)

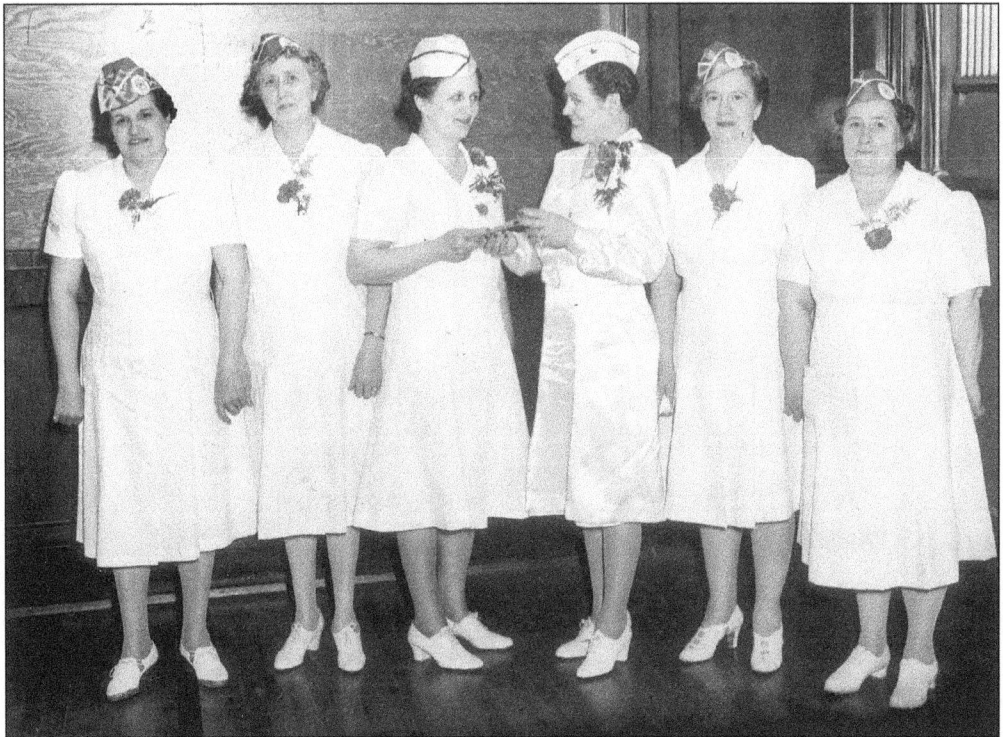

Officers of the Mothers of World War II pose for this picture at an installation ceremony. (Courtesy of Cudahy Historical Society)

Kiwanians present a skit to fellow members in 1937. Pictured are Carl Venus, John Jennejohn, Pat Furdek, Leo Joslin, Erv Budzien, Bernard Hogue, and James Gaspardo. (Courtesy of Cudahy Historical Society.)

On a tour of Miller Brewery in 1964, the Cudahy Chamber of Commerce examined old brewing tools. Pictured are (standing) Ralph Venus, Don Almon, Louis Huebler Jr., and Paul Getschman; (seated) Mayor Lawrence P. Kelly. (Courtesy of Cudahy Historical Society.)

Politicians from different levels of government came to observe Cudahy's 50th birthday in 1956. Pictured are U.S. Representative Clement Zablocki, Wisconsin State Senator Leland McParland, Justice of the Peace Peter Benka, U.S. Senator Estes Kefauver, Miss Golden Jubilee Katherine Barocci, and Mayor Vincent Totka. (Courtesy of Cudahy Historical Society.)

Miss Golden Jubilee Katherine Barocci and her court ride in the parade celebrating the city's 50th anniversary in 1956. (Courtesy of Cudahy Historical Society.)

Susan Woerfel and Frank Johnson hand out equipment to children at Lincoln School playground in 1962. The summer activity was sponsored by the Cudahy Recreation Department. (Courtesy of Cudahy Historical Society.)

These are the winners of the tricycle decorating contest sponsored by the Cudahy Safe and Sane 4th of July Association in 1961. Center is David Gazdik, and the others are unidentified. (Courtesy of Cudahy Historical Society.)

This is Sheridan Park Pool in 1937, shortly after it was built. Swimming lessons were given in the early morning, and free swim was offered until noon. In the afternoon, a fee was charged. Discount books of tickets were also offered for sale. (Courtesy of Cudahy Historical Society.)

Tom Paul sounds the gun for the start of the boys' 220-yard race for 12-13 year olds at Sheridan Park lagoon in the early 1960s. (Courtesy of Cudahy Historical Society.)

Not much is known about this photo except that it was taken at Sheridan Park, *c.* 1900. It might be a church picnic. Several of the ladies and gents are wearing hats. Note the fellow who climbed the tree in order to be in the picture. (Courtesy of Cudahy Historical Society.)

Refreshments were served to this group of bowlers in 1916, after finishing a game. (Courtesy of Cudahy Historical Society.)

Local actors, dressed in costume, appeared in a play at St. Frederick's Church hall in 1932. The actors are Joseph Wagner, Edward Stringer, James Keller, Peter Bartol, and Ervin Dretzka. (Courtesy of Cudahy Historical Society.)

A play sponsored by the Works Progress Administration (WPA) was held at St. Frederick's Church hall in 1932. These actors gathered in a classroom for this picture. The actors are (first row) unidentified, William Martin, and Dorothy Miller; (second row) two unidentified, Otto Frank, Herb Schubring, and Dr. Bernard Krueger; (third row) Milton Kerlin, Charles Cassebaum, Steve Kowalewski, James Keller, Joseph Wagner, unidentified, Alan Dement, and an unidentified person. (Courtesy of Cudahy Historical Society.)

"Stop Thief" was the name of this play staged at Kleineider's Hall in 1925. (Courtesy of Cudahy Historical Society.)

Minstrel shows were popular entertainment. This show was presented by the Kiwanis Club at St. Frederick's Church hall in the 1930s. (Courtesy of Cudahy Historical Society.)

This Indian came straight from the "wild west" to this Majestic Theater party in 1927. The sign above advertises, "Chicken Dinner candy bar: One free to each boy & girl today." (Courtesy of Cudahy Historical Society.)

This group was "dressed down" for a "hard time" party held at the American Legion hall on Packard and Barnard Avenues in 1952. (Courtesy of Cudahy Historical Society.)

DEDICATION OF PULASKI PARK — Sept. 8, 1929.
CUDAHY, WISCONSIN
Park Studio, Photo.

Pulaski Park, originally named Lindbergh Park, was purchased by the city in 1926, to serve the city's south side. It was renamed Pulaski Park at this dedication ceremony in 1929. A statue of General Pulaski, the park's namesake, was erected at the park in 1932, the same year it became a County park. (Courtesy of Cudahy Historical Society.)

Four

PROGRESS

Cudahy is not resting on its status quo. During the past ten years or so, many advancements have been made, and others are yet to come.

Open land on Pennsylvania Avenue has been developed into the Mitchell International Business Park. There are currently seven occupants with expansion room for approximately four more. They are a mixture of business and light industry.

The Creekside Drive subdivision of condominium and townhouse units north of College Avenue and west of Packard Avenue, satisfy a need for this type of dwelling in the city. Assisted living homes and several senior apartment complexes complement the housing picture.

Lakeside Commons Committee has a master plan for downtown redevelopment of Cudahy. Streetscaping—the first phase—has been completed with landscaping, benches, and brick sidewalks. Buildings on Barnard and Layton Avenues have been razed to make room for a new library, adjoining condominiums, re-routing of Barnard Avenue, a new street leading from Layton Avenue to Patrick Cudahy, Inc., and a Layton Avenue business park.

City officials, under the guidance of Mayor Raymond Glowacki and the Lakeside Commons Committee, are accomplishing these improvements. Through their efforts, the city will undergo changes that will be a source of pride for future generations.

This is Mitchell International Business Park, a Wispark-Milwaukee County venture in cooperation with the City of Cudahy. It is located on Pennsylvania Avenue, south of Layton Avenue. (Courtesy of Mayor Raymond Glowacki.)

CrossWinds Condominiums are just one example of housing units available in the Creekside Drive subdivision. There are also townhouses, duplexes, and single-family homes located there, in addition to an assisted living complex. (Courtesy of Cudahy Historical Society.)

May 15, 2001
CUDAHY PUBLIC LIBRARY
Engberg/Anderson Design Partnership, Inc.

This is an architect's version of the new Cudahy Public Library on Barnard Avenue, a major part of Cudahy's downtown redevelopment. The exterior of the one-story building is made of brick, glass, and copper, with interior accents of copper on the reference and circulation desks and light fixtures. Areas for adults, children, technology, local history, study, meeting, conference, and the "Friends of Cudahy Library" organization will be included. (Courtesy of Cudahy Public Library.)

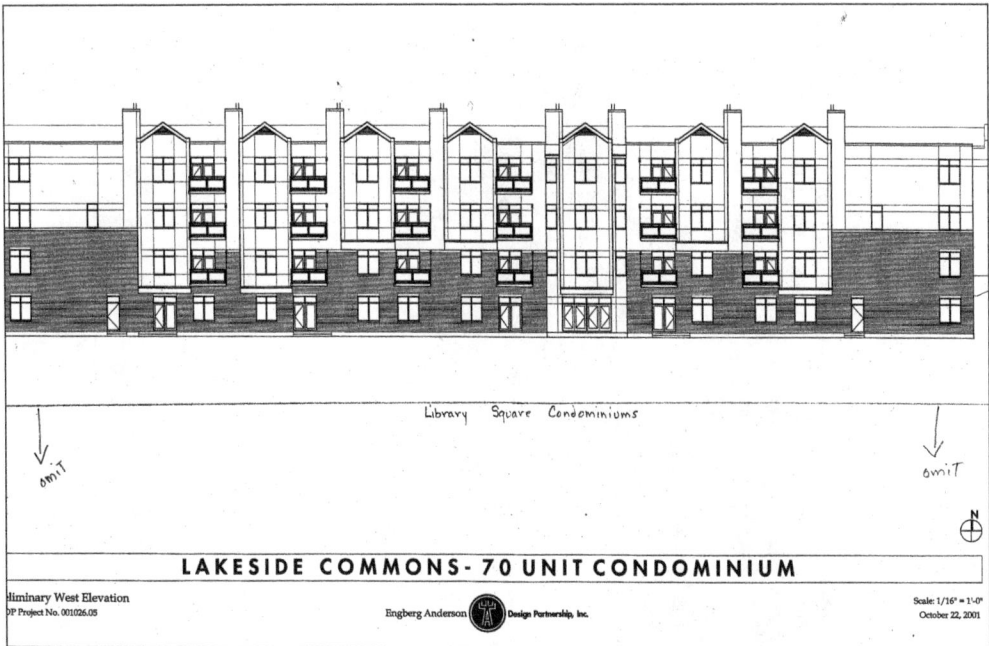

Library Square Condominiums

omit   omit

LAKESIDE COMMONS- 70 UNIT CONDOMINIUM

Preliminary West Elevation
DP Project No. 001026.05

Engberg Anderson Design Partnership, Inc.

Scale: 1/16" = 1'-0"
October 22, 2001

Library Square Condominiums will be connected to the library by an enclosed winter garden. The one or two-story units will have varied floor plans with one, two, or three bedrooms. (Courtesy of Burke Enterprises.)

These are the City Officials of 2001. Pictured are (seated) Alderpersons Bruce Schuknecht, 1st District; Ryan McCue, 2nd District; Thomas Cetnarowski, 5th District; Jill Gestwicki, 3rd District; and Sean Smith, 4th District; (standing) Philip Brannon, City Clerk/Treasurer; Raymond Glowacki, Mayor; John Zodrow, Municipal Judge; and Robert Jursik, City Attorney. (Courtesy of Mayor Raymond Glowacki.)

www.ingramcontent.com/pod-product-compliance
Lightning Source LLC
Chambersburg PA
CBHW080617110426
42813CB00006B/1530